"Rico Tice has the ability quickly to catch your attention and then lead you to face up to things that really matter in a lasting way. This book offers you a way to celebrate Christmas like never before. Let me encourage you to read *The Ultimate Christmas Wishlist*, brush aside all the extraneous Christmas tinsel, and discover the amazing gift that God is offering you. You won't regret it."

TERRY VIRGO, Founder, NewFrontiers; Author,
Life Tastes Better

"A skilled writer, Rico helps us see how the birth of Jesus means that we can know hope, peace, purpose and confidence. That is far greater than any gift we can receive on Christmas Day morning."

TONY MERIDA, Pastor, Imago Dei Church, Raleigh, NC;
Author, *Love Your Church*

"Rico has a wonderfully disarming ability to connect the good news of Jesus with real life. This book doesn't bounce off our resistant exteriors but instead gets under our skin and penetrates into our minds and hearts. Put it on your wishlist and your give-list this Christmas!"

JAGO WYNNE, Rector, Holy Trinity Clapham

"This book is ty   plicity.
This book exp   great
anecdotes, and   l but
one of them awa

GRAHAM DANIELS, G   ...ians in Sport

"Rico's writing and speaking are always the same: no fluff or hype—just the best story ever told. After an especially hope-dimming couple of years, this book will help you either discover or cherish your ultimate wishlist!"

MICHAEL HORTON, Westminster Seminary, California; Author, *Ordinary*

"Christmas, more than any other time of the year, is when we experience meaning and crave more of it, feeling like we get a small taste of life as it is meant to be. Rico Tice shows us how to enjoy the gifts of hope, peace, purpose and confidence that Jesus alone gives. Easy to read, winsome and intellectually satisfying, this is a wonderful book."

ADAM RAMSEY, Lead Pastor, Liberti Church, Gold Coast, Australia; Author, *Truth on Fire*

The
ULTIMATE
CHRISTMAS
WISHLIST

RICO TICE

thegoodbook
COMPANY

The Ultimate Christmas Wishlist
© Christianity Explored Ministries, 2022.

Published by
The Good Book Company

thegoodbook.com | thegoodbook.co.uk
thegoodbook.com.au | thegoodbook.co.nz | thegoodbook.co.in

Cover by Faceout Studio | Art direction and design by André Parker

ISBN: 9781784987701 | Printed in India

CONTENTS

CONTENTS

I. WHAT WOULD YOU LIKE FOR CHRISTMAS?

What would you like for Christmas?

I find that a difficult question to answer. But I know I do need to answer it—otherwise, it'll turn out like the year I was presented with a gift that, on unwrapping it, turned out to be a dog bowl. Which would have been great, if I'd happened to own a dog.

It's not that there's nothing I want for Christmas. The problem is with what I would like, for two reasons. Sometimes, the thing I'd like is beyond the budget of the person who's asking—I'd like a trip to the World Cup. I'd like a "top of the range" golf club. I'd like a new right knee. Other times, it's not just beyond their budget but their power. I'd like inner confidence that means I'm not knocked back by criticism and don't respond like an enraged teenager. I'd like a sense of hope for my struggling friend. I'd like peace in Afghanistan and protection for a friend of mine who works there. I'd like a guarantee that my children will grow up to enjoy wholly happy and purposeful lives.

I'd like to lose 30 pounds. It's hard to say which is least likely to happen.

But just imagine for a moment that time, budget and ability were no barrier. What would be on your ultimate Christmas wishlist? Think big. Get beyond the boxes and the socks, the books and the pyjamas, the bubble bath and the handkerchiefs. You can have anything you want.

What would you ask for?

I guess your answer will vary according to your circumstances. All of us have things at the back of our minds that we try to push to the bottom of our hearts. I've never met anyone who would finish the sentence "If I could change one thing about my life, it'd be..." with the word "nothing". For all that there is to be excited and happy about at Christmas time—the parties and the people and the food and the films—that's never the whole story. There are things we feel sad or scared or sorry about, and the presents under the tree are not going to address those. Maybe (if your aunt pointedly gives your uncle a "how to" book on home improvement again) they might even make them worse.

And so what you would most like for Christmas and what you actually get for Christmas are usually two very different things. For me, it will be socks and a book, not the World Cup trip or peace in Afghanistan. And that's ok. After all, you can't wrap up hope, or peace, or purpose, or confidence, and make a gift of them. No one can deliver those.

Except that someone did. And they did it at Christmas.

THE ARRIVAL OF JOY

At the very first Christmas, so the story goes, an angel made an announcement to some very ordinary, nondescript shepherds. This is what the angel said:

> *"I bring you good news that will cause great joy."*
> *(Bible book of Luke, chapter 2, verse 10)*

The first Christmas was about something that brought "great joy". Not polite smiles, like when I unwrapped that dog bowl, or a disappointed sigh, as may well happen this year when my wife opens my very best effort at a thoughtful, useful gift to her. No, the first Christmas was about the arrival of something that really did bring great joy.

This wasn't a joy that relied on everything in life being great; actually, it was a joy that broke into lives that were not going well. Those shepherds, and the other people who experienced the events of the first Christmas, were living in poverty and under oppression. They were subject to Roman rule—and although, when we think of the Romans, we might think of straight roads and warm baths, for 1st-century non-Roman people, their presence mainly meant sharp swords and high taxes. Things must have seemed pretty dark. Yet still the joy broke through; still these events made a difference. Here was a joy that could change even the darkest of times.

What was the source of this joy? "I bring you good news that will cause great joy," the angel said, because "you will find a baby wrapped in cloths and lying in a manger" (Luke 2 v 12). You're probably familiar with this story: Mary, Joseph, manger, shepherds, angels, wise men, baby Jesus in the manger. Children act it out every year. But somehow it's easy to end up enjoying Christmas after Christmas without ever appreciating the story's depth, its real meaning: that in the middle of the nativity scene lay a baby who brought joy—who came to give us the things that we are all looking for.

The birth of Jesus means this: that at Christmas, and in life, you can have what you would most like: hope, peace, purpose, confidence.

The aim of this book is to help you find out how.

LIGHT IN THE DARK

In the next four chapters we're going to look at those four themes, seeing who Jesus was, what he did and what difference that makes to us. First, though, we need to rewind—not 2,000 years to the very first Christmas but even further back in time, to seven centuries before Mary ever fell pregnant.

At that time, the people living in Judah—a little country on the eastern edge of the Mediterranean—

were facing an enemy as bad as, if not worse than, the Romans. Judah was facing catastrophe: invasion from the all-powerful Assyrian army. Try to imagine being in Kabul with the Taliban approaching; that's the kind of fear the people would have felt. The Assyrians were unstoppable—they were already marching through Israel, the country to Judah's north, and Judah would be next. What did the people of Judah need for Christmas? They needed peace. Protection. Rescue.

Into this moment of darkness came a message from a man who claimed to be a spokesman of God—a prophet. This man, Isaiah, was completely realistic about the dark situation Judah faced—but he had not given up hope.

"The people walking in darkness," he said, "have seen a great light; on those living in the land of deep darkness a light has dawned" (Isaiah 9 v 2).

And how would this light come? "To us a child is born, to us a son is given" (v 6).

Here is Isaiah's solution—and what he claims is God's solution—to the darkness facing Judah. A child. A baby boy.

That's it.

This is like Winston Churchill going on the radio in June 1940—when the British army was retreating from Dunkirk and Britain faced invasion and defeat by Germany—and saying, "Don't worry. Victory is secure. Hope is here. I've heard that a woman is pregnant, and she will have a son." This gift that Isaiah was announcing could not have sounded less like what the people needed. They were facing an invasion from a huge, unstoppable army. They were going to be given a tiny baby.

That's a gift that would surely have prompted a disappointed sigh at best—and more likely it would be a head-in-hands moment. The Assyrians are coming, and the answer is... a little child?!

But then Isaiah told them who this baby boy would be:

> *"To us a child is born,*
> *to us a son is given ...*
> *And he will be called*
> *Wonderful Counsellor, Mighty God,*
> *Everlasting Father, Prince of Peace." (Isaiah 9 v 6)*

Isaiah was promising the events of the first Christmas. He was describing who it was that would lie in the manger. Someone was coming who would do far more than bring rescue from an Assyrian invader—though God did also supply that.* Someone was coming who would give people what they truly wanted, were

---

* You can look up how that happened in the Old Testament book of Isaiah 37 v 36-38. The British Museum in London also has some depictions from the period of these invasions.

working for, were dreaming about: hope, peace, purpose, confidence.

YOU CAN GET WHAT YOU'D REALLY LIKE

You're probably used to hearing about the baby Jesus at Christmas. But we need to recover the shock of who this baby was and why he was born. The claim of the Bible is that the one whose birth the angel announced and whose identity Isaiah described is still, even all these years later, all anyone needs to ask for.

The Bible is realistic about life: that there are as many things that take joy as give it—that the things we most want out of life often elude us. But the Bible is also very clear about where to find the things we most want and need. They can be found in the baby who was born at the first Christmas: the boy who was the Mighty God, the Prince of Peace, the Everlasting Father, and the Wonderful Counsellor.

I don't expect you to believe that just because I say it. In fact, please don't believe it just because I say it! Instead, I'd love you to spend some time with me, in the next few chapters, looking at some of the evidence for that claim. We're going to focus not on the baby Jesus but the adult Jesus (because, as for all of us, his birth was only the beginning!). We'll see how Jesus grew up to say he was and show he was the Mighty God, the Prince of Peace, the Everlasting Father and the Wonderful Counsellor. And as we do so, you can consider for yourself who Jesus is. You can see how, if he is who he claims to be, the ultimate Christmas wishlist—the hope, the peace, the purpose and the confidence that we're all searching for—is wrapped up in him.

Here's the claim: that in Jesus, you get what you would really like in life—that this Christmas, in a profound and lasting way, what you most need and what you actually get can be the same thing.

Could it be true?

2. HOPE

For me, it's always been when the lights and decorations go up in the shops—that's when I get excited about Christmas. Other people complain about commercialisation when the shops get Christmassy in October—but I love it. I see the decorations go up and I start to look forward: Christmas is coming.

That feeling of looking forward to something good, something better, is what we usually call hope. And there are few emotions more powerful. When you have hope, even if your life remains the same for now, you go about your day smiling inside; it changes you. Hope gives you an expectation that the future is worth working for and worth waiting for—even if, like Christmas Day when you're a child, that future seems to come very, very slowly!

Hope drives us—until it disappoints us. We all know what it's like to have our hopes dashed. It's the sinking feeling when the Christmas present that you've saved up for and planned carefully turns out to be out of stock and unavailable till the first Monday in January. More seriously, it's the gut-punch you experience when the application gets rejected, or the person you really like tells you that they're just not into you, or the sale falls through, or the test results come back, and all your happy daydreams dissolve in a moment.

Perhaps you know how it feels when you do get what you've been dreaming of, only to find that it's not all you thought it would be. You finally get the job, or the relationship, or the retirement that you'd been hoping for and... it just doesn't deliver the satisfaction it promised. Sometimes, Christmas is like that. I remember one year ages ago when my mum, who managed to organise everything (and everyone) through December while also working very hard as a nurse, got to Christmas Day, was spoken to unkindly by a relative, and told me that evening, "What was said just ruined the day for me". She'd worked so hard to make Christmas wonderful, and then... it wasn't.

And when our hopes are disappointed, we tend to set our sights on something else, and the whole cycle starts over again. But sometimes we get knocked down too low for too long, and we end up with no hope at all, and we're just left with the feeling that there's nothing to look forward to.

To have hope is to feel happy—not in a fleeting way but in a lasting one. It's a wonderful gift. But for hope to be worth having, it needs to deliver what it promises. There's no point in spending your life hoping for something that never arrives, or that disappoints, or that fades. Many people are more aware of this at Christmas than any other time of year. I don't just mean not getting the gifts you wanted. Christmas can also provide a bitter reminder that this year didn't deliver what you'd hoped for and that next year might not either. December can be the best of times, but it can also be the worst of times.

Sadly, finding real hope—hope that lasts, hope that comes true—proves elusive to many of us. But it is this kind of real hope that the Christian faith claims that Jesus offers.

What are you hoping in and hoping for? Perhaps so far in life all your hopes have been fulfilled, or perhaps they've been shattered. More likely, you've experienced a bit of both. But whoever you are, whatever you've experienced in the past and whatever your life is like in the present, Christianity is an invitation to put your hope in a future that is better than anything else you could imagine—and more certain than any other promise you could hear.

To show you the kind of hope that Jesus was born to bring, I want to take you back to a single day in Jesus' adult life. We're going to look briefly at three snapshots from that one day, as told to us in one of the four Gospels, or historical biographies, in the Bible. The one we're focusing on here was written by a man called

Luke, a doctor, who interviewed eyewitnesses of what Jesus said and did, and wrote it up in around AD 60, well within living memory of the events he describes.

STORM ON THE SEA

The first incident takes place on the lake of Galilee in northern Israel—a lake so big it's often called a sea:

> *"One day Jesus said to his disciples, 'Let us go over to the other side of the lake.' So they got into a boat and set out. As they sailed, he fell asleep. A squall came down on the lake, so that the boat was being swamped, and they were in great danger.*
>
> *"The disciples went and woke him, saying, 'Master, Master, we're going to drown!'*
>
> *"He got up and rebuked the wind and the raging waters; the storm subsided, and all was calm. 'Where is your faith?' he asked his disciples.*
>
> *"In fear and amazement they asked one another, 'Who is this? He commands even the winds and the water, and they obey him.'"* (Luke 8 v 22-25)

Imagine the desperation of Jesus' friends, the disciples, as their routine boat trip turns into a life-threatening emergency. This is not just your average storm. In fact it's more like a hurricane, caused by cold air from the mountains meeting the warm air around the Sea of Galilee and producing a typhoon-like weather system on the surface of the water.

When woken up to be faced with the horrors of this hurricane, what does Jesus do? He stands up and says, *Quiet, be still*.

And it is.

Here is a man with the power to control the uncontrollable—a man who can take a hopeless situation and turn it around completely. The wind and the waves don't have ears, and yet when Jesus speaks, he can calm them. So the disciples are left asking the right question: "Who is this?"

Who can do something like that? What category do you put him in? If he can calm a storm with a word, he's clearly not simply a teacher or a philosopher or a healer. Who is he?

This matters to us because it's not just about seas and storms and fishing boats. It's about the things that keep you awake at night because they're out of your control, the question marks that cloud your future, the hard things that threaten to overwhelm you. Wouldn't it be amazing news if there were someone with the power to control those things? It wouldn't make hard things easy, but it would be deeply reassuring if we could know that behind the universe stands someone who is running the show and working things out. The kind of someone, in fact, that Isaiah promised when he spoke about the baby who would be born at the first Christmas—when he called him "Mighty God".

I wonder if those words were circling in the disciples' minds as they asked each other, "Who is this?" Could this man be the promised Mighty God, walking on the earth he had created and commanding it with his words?

TERROR ON THE BEACH

Maybe, though, the disciples might have thought that the calming of the storm was a stroke of luck—a happy coincidence, a one-off. So, let's look at a second snapshot from that day. As the boat reaches the shore, Jesus and his friends set foot on land. There they are confronted by someone for whom hope has vanished and the thought of happiness is little more than a bad joke. Just to warn you, this part is not very warm and Christmassy.

> "When Jesus stepped ashore, he was met by a
> demon-possessed man from the town. For a long
> time this man had not worn clothes or lived in a
> house, but had lived in the tombs. When he saw
> Jesus, he cried out and fell at his feet, shouting
> at the top of his voice, 'What do you want with
> me, Jesus, Son of the Most High God? I beg you,
> don't torture me!' For Jesus had commanded the
> impure spirit to come out of the man. Many times
> it had seized him, and though he was chained hand
> and foot and kept under guard, he had broken his
> chains and had been driven by the demon into
> solitary places." (Luke 8 v 27-29)

I wonder what you make of this idea of demon possession. Is there really such a thing? Surely that's an idea from another era—a less enlightened age?

To that I would say: what about the idea of evil? Is there such a thing as that? Perhaps we should ask the family of Sarah Everard, the London woman who was murdered in 2021 by an off-duty policeman pretending to carry out policing duties, or the families of all the women who have been murdered—even just in London—since then. Read some newspapers next time someone does something truly awful and you'll easily observe that some acts are so bad that "evil" really is the only word that fits them. But then we can't help but ask the unsettling question of where evil comes from. Is it just a case of bad choices or bad education or bad parenting?

The reality is that every day, we all experience impulses inside us and influences around us that drag us down—maybe not into what we would call evil but certainly into harshness, meanness and even cruelty. And the Bible says that there's a spiritual being who stands behind and ignites those impulses and influences. He's called the devil, and his foot soldiers are demons. They hate God; they hate good; they hate joy. They are opposed to human happiness. This man on the beach is a picture of their great desire to bring misery: they've driven him outside of society and away from those who love him, so that he's alone among the tombs. His life is utterly miserable. There's no doubt about it: he is a victim of true evil.

Everyone responds to what I've just said about evil and the devil in one of two ways because there are only two things we can do with this. One is to deny the devil is real and to live as though what you see is all there is. But then it becomes hard to explain the reality of evil when we see it at its worst. The other response is to be deeply afraid of it—if you know there's evil and that it's more powerful than you, you will live in fear of it.

Denial or fear. Those are the two responses to the reality of evil—until Jesus shows up. Jesus doesn't deny evil, and he isn't afraid of evil. Instead, he removes it.

> *"Jesus asked him, 'What is your name?'*
>
> *"'Legion,' he replied, because many demons had gone into him. And they begged Jesus repeatedly not to order them to go into the Abyss.*
>
> *"A large herd of pigs was feeding there on the hillside. The demons begged Jesus to let them go into the pigs, and he gave them permission. When the demons came out of the man, they went into the pigs, and the herd rushed down the steep bank into the lake and was drowned.*
>
> *"When those tending the pigs saw what had happened, they ran off and reported this in the*

> *town and countryside, and the people went out to*
> *see what had happened. When they came to Jesus,*
> *they found the man from whom the demons had*
> *gone out, sitting at Jesus' feet, dressed and in his*
> *right mind." (Luke 8 v 30-35)*

The man who started that day alone, broken and distressed, and heading for the same fate as those pigs ends up "sitting at Jesus' feet, dressed and in his right mind". This man, who has been beyond hope, gets a happy ending. He can return to his family and friends. He's restored, whole and happy. And all because he's had an encounter with Jesus.

Who is Jesus? Could we be looking at the Mighty God, who has come to earth with the power to defeat evil?

And still Jesus' day isn't done.

GRIEF IN THE TOWN

Nothing robs us of joy like the grief of losing the people we love. The presence of grief means that happiness can never be undiluted. Even on our best days—even on Christmas Day—there'll always be a feeling of "Oh, if only X had been here to enjoy this".

In the next scene Jesus meets the most desperate grief. As he leaves the beach and walks into the nearest town, he meets a local dignitary.

> *"A man named Jairus, a synagogue leader, came*
> *and fell at Jesus' feet, pleading with him to come to*

> *his house because his only daughter, a girl of about*
> *twelve, was dying." (Luke 8 v 41-42)*

Jairus is about to lose his beloved daughter, and there's nothing he can do. He knows his wife will never quite smile in the same way again—and neither will he. He's heard this man has miraculous powers. So he throws himself at Jesus' feet, and he begs for help. Jesus says he'll come, and they set out for Jairus' house together, but there's a delay on the way and before they can reach the sickbed of the dying girl, Jairus hears the horrific words that every parent dreads:

> *"Someone came from the house of Jairus, the*
> *synagogue leader. 'Your daughter is dead,' he said.*
> *'Don't bother the teacher anymore.'" (Luke 8 v 49)*

It's a punch in the stomach. All Jairus's worst nightmares have come true.

But then Jesus speaks:

> *"Don't be afraid; just believe, and she will be*
> *healed." (Luke 8 v 50)*

Just believe? She will be healed? This is a big claim—a serious claim. When someone's lost a child, you don't play games with the parents. The stakes are high now. Jesus had better be able to deliver.

> *"When he arrived at the house of Jairus, he did*
> *not let anyone go in with him except Peter, John*

> *and James, and the child's father and mother.*
> *Meanwhile, all the people were wailing and*
> *mourning for her. 'Stop wailing,' Jesus said. 'She is*
> *not dead but asleep.'*
>
> *"They laughed at him, knowing that she was dead."*
> *(Luke 8 v 51-53)*

This is a contemptuous laugh of disbelief at what has just been said. *Who do you think you are? She's dead! Don't dangle this false hope in front of these poor parents.*

But it's not false hope:

> *"[Jesus] took her by the hand and said, 'My child,*
> *get up!' Her spirit returned, and at once she stood*
> *up." (Luke 8 v 54-55)*

Jesus can raise a child from death just as easily as you or I might rouse a child from sleep. He has the authority to turn chaos into calm, the power to remove evil, and the ability to turn grief into joy. What category is big enough for him?

Luke is showing us, here and throughout his biography of Jesus, that there's only one category big enough: Mighty God.

OUT THERE AND DOWN HERE

I don't know if you believe there's a God out there. Many of us like to think that there is. Or, at the very least, we like to think there's something more than our material universe: some bigger reality that makes sense of the story of life on earth. But have you ever said to yourself, "If there is a God out there, it would be great if he proved it"?

In the life of Jesus, we see that God has. And Jesus doesn't only show us that is someone out there; he also shows us what kind of someone there is out there. There's a Mighty God, who gets involved in his creation, who's interested in the details of our lives, and who cares about our joys and our tears. He cares about this world—that's why he came to it at the first Christmas.

This means that we're right to hope for more, for better. If this is what God is like—if the Bible's description of him is true—then the reality is that we were actually made to enjoy a life without storms, without evil and without death. And we can have that life. The Bible tells a unique story about where the world is heading. It says that one day the Mighty God will come to earth again, and when he does, everything that he did on a local, individual level 2,000 years ago he will do on a global, cosmic level. The calming of the storm, the rescuing of the man and the raising of the girl are like a thumbnail preview of an entirely new world: a world where all the uncertainties will be brought under control, a world where evil will not intrude, and a world without sickness or grief or death.

That is the world that, deep down, we're all longing for. It's what we glimpse in the best bits of the best

Christmasses—the laughter, the joy, the together-ness and the rest. It's what we miss when December proves hard. But at the first Christmas, Jesus came to give us real hope: the knowledge that there will come a tomorrow when things are not just better but completely, flawlessly perfect.

In one sense, having this hope changes nothing; and yet, at the same time, it changes everything. We may still experience darkness in this life—disappoint-ment, divorce, depression or disease. But we can travel through sadness without despair because with Jesus, the worst thing is never the last thing. There's always hope. And having this hope means that we can enjoy the good things, the smaller hopes—fun, food, family, fitness, friendships, falling in love—without that nagging fear of losing them someday, because we know that even sweeter days lie ahead.

This is hope—real hope. This is what allows you to go about smiling inside, whatever your day brings. This is what the Mighty God was born at the first Christmas to invite you to enjoy.

3. PEACE

It's possibly the most famous sports match of all time.

On Christmas Day 1914, with the First World War a few months old, British and German soldiers on the front lines in France left their trenches, met up in the no man's land between them, and had a kickabout with a football. (The result is unrecorded—but rumours are the Germans won on penalties.) It was a glorious moment of peace in the midst of one of the most brutal wars ever fought.

And that's why it's remembered. This brief interlude of friendship stands out because it was so abnormal and unexpected. Even as it happened, elsewhere along the line the guns were firing, and men were dying. Nothing of its kind happened on any of the other three Christmas Days during the First World War. It hasn't happened since, either. Despite John Lennon declaring in his 1971 Christmas song that "war is over", it actually wasn't, and it still really isn't. There hasn't been a Christmas Day in this century or the last in which there has been peace all around the world. Humans often seem better at fighting than friendship.

And yet still we long for peace. Still we imagine how great it would be, as Lennon did in another of his songs, to see all people living life in peace.

Wouldn't it be wonderful, this Christmas, to see peace *out there*—an end to the conflicts and crises around the globe that have been all over the news for so much of the year? Wouldn't it be glorious if the guns really did fall silent and never started up again?

Wouldn't it be wonderful if peace could be a reality *in here*, too? While at one level we enjoy the anticipation of Christmas, many of us also long for a break from the stress that seems to accompany us through most of December as Christmas Day rushes towards us. Even in less busy months, we long for an end to the anxious soundtrack of thoughts that play in our mind like a record on repeat, or for a solution to the regrets and responsibilities that keep us awake at night.

And wouldn't it be great if there could be peace *between us*, in our relationships? I'm sure that, like mine, your circle of family and friends has been marred by relational strife over the years. It may be that you'll spend Christmas walking a diplomatic tightrope in order to keep family members from falling out, or struggling with the distance that has grown between you and a child or a parent or a friend. There's a reason why January is the busiest month for divorces—people spend a few days trying to get on with their nearest and no-longer-dearest, and by New Year, they can't see a way to do it anymore.

The absence of peace is so painful—it's gaping silences and raised voices and lingering regrets. But the presence of peace... Well, that's truly beautiful. It's wholeness and harmony. It's completeness, tranquillity, security and safety.

That's precisely the vision behind the Bible's word for peace: *shalom*. It paints a picture of a peace that is deeper and more far-reaching than the awkward ceasefires we often settle for. Shalom is not just "I get along with my neighbour; we don't hassle each other, and we leave each other to get on with our lives". That would be all right. But shalom is better: it's "I take delight in my neighbour. We so enjoy each other that we take down the fence between each other's gardens; we babysit each other's kids; we go for a walk together after Christmas lunch, and we spend Boxing Day together, and we love it."

Is there any real hope of a world like that? A world of kickabouts instead of conflicts?

Yes. But first we need to understand why peace so often eludes us.

THE PROBLEM IN MY JOURNAL

When I was a teenage, I kept a journal. I wrote it because I thought I was such a great guy that I owed it to humanity to record my life. The only problem was that, week after week, it showed that I was the opposite of great. I'd lament that there was a lack of world peace, but there was no evidence in my journal that I ever laid aside the weapons of malice and sarcasm myself. I'd say, "Wouldn't it be great if the starving were fed?" and then I'd ask my parents for a bigger allowance, and I'd eat it. I'd mention wanting to do things with my sister's friends that would have horrified me if my friends had wanted to do them with my sister.

Looking back on it, my journal reveals that there was a problem in my world, and that problem was me. This was probably already obvious to the people around me, but when I realized it, it was a real turning point.

And this is not only my problem—it's the same for each one of us. Have you noticed that though we want to be at peace, we humans are the ones who spoil the peace? On a global level and on a personal level, wherever you have conflict, you'll find it was a human who started it. Why? Because while we all want peace, we also all want to be the ones to dictate the peace treaty. Deep down, we expect every relationship to be on our terms. Most of our frustrations, tensions and arguments with others arise at least in part because other people don't do what we want them to do. If we were to keep a journal, we'd find that there was a slogan for our lives: "My life, my rules".

I'm not saying we're all selfish and self-centred all of the time—we're capable of great generosity too. Even teenage Rico had some good points! But in your more honest moments, you'll be aware that there's something inside you which means you are sometimes selfish, or unthoughtful, or even deliberately nasty. That's why we hurt even the people we love most: because something inside us is saying, "My life, my rules". And that's why our hopes for peace are never totally fulfilled.

But it gets worse.

CHOOSING CONFLICT

If you really want to understand what's wrong, you need to see that the problem is not just horizontal—it's not just broken peace out there, in here and between us. The Bible's diagnosis of the root of the problem is vertical. We're saying, "My life, my rules" to God, not just to each other. God made everything and sustains everything, so you might think we'd say, "Your world, your rules". But instead, people live as though God should abide by their rules and fit in with their plans. They choose conflict with him instead of peace with him. That attitude is what the Bible calls "sin", and sin matters more than you might think—because it matters very greatly to God.

Sin has consequences, because God is a God of justice, and so he judges sin. This is good news when we are the victims of sin. God is not indifferent to justice—as

33

we've seen, he does not run away from evil, and he does not wink at abuse. God cares. I've been the victim of real malice at a couple of points in my life, and I take comfort in knowing that injustice matters to God as much as it matters to me. If you have been the victim of sin, then you can know that God does care and God will do something about it.

So God's justice is a comfort; but it is also a challenge because the truth is that while some of us may be victims, all of us are rebels. There is no one who has never said, "My life, my rules". What I do to you matters to God, and what you do to me matters to God, and how we treat the world matters to God. And so we face the consequences of our sin: the justice of God.

Jesus himself pictured those consequences in terms of darkness. He spoke of a place beyond death—a place of "darkness, where there will be weeping and gnashing of teeth" (Matthew 8 v 12). Imagine a life spent in constant darkness, with no light whatsoever and no hope of ever having any. A life beyond death, without hope or peace or purpose or confidence, and with only tears and regret for company. Jesus called that place "hell".

The Bible is very straight with us: if we turn our backs on the Lord of light, we'll find ourselves left in the dark. God will hand us over to the consequences that our conflict with him and our treatment of others deserves.

But there is hope. Remember Isaiah's promise: "The people walking in darkness have seen a great light ... to us a child is born, to us a son is given ... And he will be called ... Mighty God ... Prince of Peace" (Isaiah 9 v 2, 6). If you want to find peace with God, now and for ever, Jesus is the place to look.

Although when he lived on earth, it didn't seem like that.

THREE STEPS TO PARADISE

For a Prince of Peace, Jesus really did make a lot of people angry. The religious and political rulers of the day had a problem with him because he didn't fit in with their rules, their agenda or their priorities. They saw Jesus as a threat to their power, and so they were determined to have him killed. They conspired with the Roman government to have Jesus arrested in secret, condemned in a sham trial and executed in public. The charge: claiming to be God. The sentence: death by crucifixion—an absolutely brutal method of capital punishment. And so the one who was laid in a wooden manger when he was born was now nailed to a wooden cross to die.

But he wasn't the only one facing execution that day:

> *"Two other men, both criminals, were also led out with [Jesus] to be executed. When they came to the place called the Skull, they crucified him there, along with the criminals—one on his right, the other on his left ...*

"One of the criminals who hung there hurled insults at him: 'Aren't you the Messiah? Save yourself and us!'

"But the other criminal rebuked him. 'Don't you fear God,' he said, 'since you are under the same sentence? We are punished justly, for we are getting what our deeds deserve. But this man has done nothing wrong.'

"Then he said, 'Jesus, remember me when you come into your kingdom.' Jesus answered him, 'Truly I tell you, today you will be with me in paradise.'"
(Luke 23 v 32-33, 39-43)

"Today you will be with me in paradise." When you think about it, that's an outrageous offer. This criminal is under the sentence of death. He's most likely a murderer and a terrorist. He's been cast out of society and nailed up on a cross to slowly suffocate to death.

Yet what does Jesus promise him? A place of peace. That's what the word "paradise" is getting at. It implies harmony, wholeness and tranquillity.

How can one dying man look across at another dying man and make such a promise?

In the verses leading up to that peace offer, there are three key moments. Think of them as three steps to paradise.

Step 1 is in verses 41-42. "Don't you fear God?" the criminal says. "We are punished justly, for we are getting what our deeds deserve."

He doesn't say, *I'm a victim*. He doesn't say, *I'm innocent*. It's as if the journal of his life has been opened, and his heart has been exposed. There's a problem in his world, and he knows that that problem is him. He says, *I deserve to be here. I'm being punished justly, not only by the arm of the state but by the arm of God*. He acknowledges his wrongdoing. I don't meet many people this honest about their own flaws! But I wish I did—because that's the first step.

I don't know what you made of all the talk of sin and judgment earlier on in this chapter. I realise that our culture finds it unpalatable. But the thing is that Christianity will never make sense until you get to the point where you look at your wrongdoing and say, "Actually, I've been living with a 'My life, my rules' attitude, and I deserve judgment."

The other criminal mocked Jesus, but his sneering couldn't change the truth of what he'd done. Today, too, Western culture laughs at sin. "What does it matter?" we say. But this can't change the truth either. Our conflict with God is real, it's serious, and it's our fault. Admitting this is actually wonderfully freeing—because it means we're able to recognise who Jesus is and what we need from him.

And this is *Step 2*—recognising that Jesus is the King, the Mighty God, who has come to earth. That's what that criminal does—he sees that "this man has done nothing wrong" (v 41), and then he says, "Jesus, remember me when you come into your kingdom" (v 42). When he looks at Jesus, he doesn't see a desperate man at the end of his life but a man who's in charge of a kingdom. He sees a king—a king who can calm a storm, who can defeat evil, who can raise the dead, and who will "come into" his kingdom even though he is about to die.

And so—and this is *Step 3*—this dying man cries out to Jesus for rescue: "Jesus, remember me when you come into your kingdom."

The criminal doesn't just want Jesus to think of him fondly: "remember me" means he wants Jesus to act for him. Think of a married couple. If one of them says, "Remember, darling, it's our anniversary next week", they're not expecting their partner merely to remember that fact but to do something about it—to book the table or buy the flowers. This criminal sees that Jesus has a kingdom beyond death—and when Jesus gets there, the man wants Jesus to act for him. He asks Jesus to welcome him, a condemned criminal, into that place of peace. This criminal offers nothing, but he asks for everything.

What does Jesus say in response? Well, he doesn't say, *Sorry—I can't help you.*

He doesn't say, *I'll tell you how you can save yourself. Live a decent life, say your prayers, love your neighbour and go to church, and then you'll book your place in heaven.*

He doesn't say, *You decided to reject me and my rule in your life. You made your bed, and now you'll lie in it.*

No—Jesus says, "Truly I tell you, today you will be

with me in paradise". No conditions, no qualifications, no delays: just total acceptance, total forgiveness and total peace with God.

The criminal offers nothing, but he receives everything—for free.

SHATTERED

Yet, while this forgiveness is free for the criminal, it isn't really free at all: it costs Jesus his life.

> "It was now about noon, and darkness came over the whole land until three in the afternoon, for the sun stopped shining ... Jesus called out with a loud voice, 'Father, into your hands I commit my spirit.' When he had said this, he breathed his last."
>
> (Luke 23 v 44-46)

This three-hour period of total darkness in the middle of the day was not an eclipse. It was a supernatural sign—a sign of God's judgment against sin. Yet this judgment didn't fall on the people who deserved it. They didn't die in the darkness—Jesus did.

In a world of conflict and rebellion, Jesus was the only person always to have kept the peace. If Jesus had kept a journal, you wouldn't find any wrongdoing in it. No rebellion against God, no selfishness towards other people—never a moment of grumbling or greed. Yet on the cross, he experienced God's judgment. As Jesus hung there dying, God was handing him over to the consequences of other people's sin. Of my sin. Jesus was paying for all the wrong I recorded in my journal. My sinful record had become his.

And Jesus paid that price willingly so that he could offer peace.

A few years ago, as I was cycling in London, my front wheel jammed between the bars of a road drain. The bike stopped dead, I flew over the handlebars, and I hit the surface of the road head first. If I hadn't been wearing a helmet, I would probably have been killed, according to the doctor I saw afterwards. But I was wearing a helmet. It was smashed to pieces, but I just stood up. I was shaken but basically fine. Because of the helmet, I was alive.

Bicycle helmets are designed to absorb the energy of an impact so that it's not transmitted to your head. In order to absorb a serious impact, though, the internal structure of the helmet has to shatter. So when I crashed, my helmet was wrecked by the impact that otherwise would have killed me. And that is a small and inadequate picture of what Jesus did on the cross. Here was God himself, taking his own judgment, bearing his own anger, taking into himself the darkness that should be mine. He was shattered so that I would be safe.

EVERYTHING CHANGES

The Prince of Peace was born at the first Christmas so he could die on the first Good Friday. We won't understand why Jesus came unless we understand why he died. He experienced the darkness of judgment so that the criminal next to him, and anyone else who asks, would not have to endure it; and so that he, and we, could instead enter into God's place of peace for eternity. Peace with God is what Jesus offered the criminal, and peace with God is what he continues to offer today. The steps to peace haven't changed. If we acknowledge our wrongdoing, accept Jesus as King, and ask him to rescue us, then we too can know peace. That's all we have to do—but we do have to do it.

I mentioned earlier that a major turning point in my life was looking through my journal and realising that the problem in my life was *me*. It was a turning point because it was the first of those three steps to paradise. In the end, I took Jesus up on his offer.

And when we do that, everything changes.

It changes things *in here*—inside. Having peace with God means you can face the world with joy and confidence because you're at peace with the one who owns the place! When you mess up, you don't need to try to ignore it, or seek to hide it, or work to excuse it. You can be honest. This is wonderfully freeing.

It changes things *between us*. God's Spirit gets to work in the lives of his people, repairing broken relationships and making friends out of enemies. Because we know how much we have been forgiven by God, we can learn to forgive others. We're able to say those two phrases that are so crucial to relational harmony: "I'm sorry—I was wrong" and "I forgive you". That won't always be easy, it won't always look perfect and it will often take time, but God's peace does give us real hope for all our relationships. In most families, for Christmas to work, at least one person in the house has to be able to resist the temptation to explode, and then be able to forgive and to move on, and the Spirit works in people to enable them to do this.

And one day, there'll be peace out there. There's hope for our bitter and broken world. History is heading somewhere good. There will be a day when the Prince of Peace will restore the whole creation to a state of shalom—of real peace—fully and finally and for ever.

All that is possible because Jesus, the Mighty God, is also the Prince of Peace. His death means that as we look at the journal of our lives and see the evidence of our sin, we can say to him with confidence, "I'm sorry—I was wrong". And in return, we can hear with comfort, *I forgive you. You will be with me in paradise.*

4. PURPOSE

Have you heard of Blue Monday? Maybe not—but you've probably experienced it. It's the third Monday in January, and it's reputed to be the least joyful day of the year. Christmas is over. The credit-card bills are dropping, the post-festive-food diet is under way, the batteries in the presents need replacing, the New Year resolutions need replacing too, and it's still dark outside. The mad rush for Christmas Day is done. The fun of New Year is past. All that effort, and still January comes, and still it feels the same as the last one did and the next one will. The thing about Christmas is that it doesn't really change anything—apart from your bank balance. On Blue Monday, people find themselves wondering, "What was it all for?"

The third Monday in January is not, of course, the only time people feel that way. Not long ago, I went to a school reunion. I found myself in conversation with an old schoolmate, and we replayed for each other the 35 years since we'd left school. My friend was brutally honest: "I've spent my life just going from one thing to another," he said. "I've just lived." It felt to him like it had been a bit empty—like it had been a bit of an anticlimax. What was it all *for*?

I remember feeling something similar myself when I was clearing out my parents' house after they'd died. They'd had full lives, good lives. The house was full of the signs of two lives well lived. But as I looked around at all the trophies won, all the milestones marked and all the Christmases celebrated, I just thought, "What did it matter?" The reality of death suddenly made the preceding eight decades of life seem strangely meaningless. My parents were here, and then they weren't. What was it all *for*?

Here is the problem. All of us hope that our lives mean something. We want to make a difference, to leave a legacy, to build something worthwhile. Having a sense of purpose in life is what gets us out of bed in the morning and what pulls us through the tough times. But what actually is your purpose, beyond just living? And if you find one, can it survive you eventually dying? The fact is that things end. Christmas comes and goes. Seasons of life pass us by. And life itself flickers and ultimately fades. It sounds depressing, but it's true. As clearing out my parents' house showed me, death mocks everything we achieve and accomplish and accumulate.

And that's why every culture in history has had to find a way to deal with the reality of death.

Here's how 21st-century Western societies do it. First, we deny it. We just pretend it's not there. Near where I live, there's a great playground. My kids love it. For centuries, though, there was a cemetery on that site, right in the middle of the community. But then they moved the cemetery miles away, behind a high wall, away from sight, and they've put a playground in instead. It's symbolic of what we do with death as a culture. We hide it. We pretend it won't happen.

Second, we try to downplay it. Think of all the ways in which we describe death to make it sound less final— less of a full stop. We pass away. We go upstairs. We fall off our perch or shuffle off this mortal coil. We become an angel in heaven or a star in the sky. Anything to stop it sounding so final. We like it when we read Professor Dumbledore remarking, in one of J.K. Rowling's Harry Potter books, that "To the well-organized mind, death is but the next great adventure".

But then reality intrudes. We go to a colleague's funeral. A loved one dies. We ourselves get a terminal diagnosis. We can't deny death's reality any longer or downplay how much it hurts. Death is not an adventure for those left behind—it's agony! Death robs us of our loved ones—and people like that, people who love us and are always there for us, are hard to come by.

When we have to confront that reality, all that's left is to start to despair about death, because death drains life of meaning. John-Paul Sartre, the 20th-century atheist philosopher, was commendably unafraid of looking at the reality of death and drawing the logical conclusions of his beliefs. He wrote in his novel *Nausea*:

> *"Nothing happens while you live. The scenery changes, people come in and go out, that's all. There are no beginnings. Days are tacked on to days without rhyme or reason, an interminable monotonous addition."*

That's what Sartre thought—but few of us want him to be right! Not many people really want to live as though there is no real reason for existing, no meaning to be found in all our successes and struggles.

Yet if life ends with death, then Sartre is right. So to find meaning in life, we need an answer to death.

NO BODY

By the end of the day we call Good Friday, Jesus seemed like the last place to look for any answers when it comes to death. He had made some big claims, he had achieved some notable things, he had stirred up hopes and dreams... and then he had died. His body was laid in a tomb, and a huge stone was rolled over the entrance. It was all over.

That was Friday. But Sunday was coming... and the belief at the heart of the Christian faith is that on that Sunday morning, something extraordinary happened:

something that can rob death of its power and give life the purpose we long for.

Here's how the final chapter of Luke's Gospel begins:

"On the first day of the week, very early in the morning, the women took the spices they had prepared and went to the tomb." (Luke 24 v 1)

Can you imagine what these friends of Jesus were feeling as they hurried to his tomb on that Sunday morning? I would guess it was a mixture of grief at the death of their friend, fear of the authorities who had killed him, and hopelessness because they'd dared to hope that this particular friend was in fact the Mighty God and the Prince of Peace, but now he was lying cold and lifeless, enclosed behind a massive stone. Everything seemed to have gone wrong.

But to this grief, fear and hopelessness is about to be added shock.

"They found the stone rolled away from the tomb, but when they entered, they did not find the body of the Lord Jesus. While they were wondering about this, suddenly two men in clothes that gleamed like lightning stood beside them. In their fright the women bowed down with their faces to the ground, but the men said to them, 'Why do you look for the living among the dead? He is not here; he has risen! Remember how he told you, while he was still with you in Galilee: "The

Son of Man must be delivered over to the hands
of sinners, be crucified and on the third day be
raised again."' Then they remembered his words."
(Luke 24 v 2-8)

No stone at the entrance. No body in the tomb. And two angels appearing in clothes that gleam like lightning. (If you're at a loss at the mention of angels, you aren't alone—the women fall flat on their faces when they encounter them. They know this is not normal.)

And then comes the news that is going to change their lives for ever—that's going to change the world for ever. Seven little words: "He is not here; he has risen!"

Jesus is alive.

That's the declaration that lies at the heart of Christianity, and on which the whole of the Christian faith stands or collapses: Jesus died and then came back to life.

EVIDENCE OR PREJUDICE?

If you find this very hard to believe, I'm not surprised. It's hard to believe that a man rose from the dead. It just doesn't happen. And people in those days knew that:

"When [the women] came back from the tomb, they
told all these things to the Eleven [the disciples]
and to all the others ... But they did not believe the
women, because their words seemed to them like
nonsense." (Luke 24 v 9, 11)

None of Jesus' friends leapt to illogical conclusions. First-century people knew just as well as we do that dead people do not rise—it's against the laws of nature.

And yet... in the space of a few weeks, those same men who had dismissed the resurrection as nonsense were proclaiming that Jesus was alive—that God had reversed the laws of nature and raised his Son from the dead. In the space of a few decades, Christianity went from being the niche beliefs of a handful of men and women in Jerusalem to something embraced by thousands of people across the ancient world. In time, this tiny start-up religion ended up shaking the entire Roman Empire. And in those same decades, ten of Jesus' eleven closest followers died because they claimed Jesus had risen. So seriously did they take the claim that Jesus was alive that they were willing to be killed for it.

So what had changed? What caused this huge paradigm shift, so that they went from dismissing the resurrection as nonsense to giving up their lives for it?

Here's what happened next, that same Sunday evening, as the disciples were gathering together.

> "Jesus himself stood among them and said to them, 'Peace be with you.'
>
> "They were startled and frightened, thinking they saw a ghost. He said to them, 'Why are you troubled, and why do doubts rise in your minds?

*Look at my hands and my feet. It is I myself! Touch
me and see; a ghost does not have flesh and bones,
as you see I have.'*

"*When he had said this, he showed them his hands
and feet. And while they still did not believe it
because of joy and amazement, he asked them,
'Do you have anything here to eat?' They gave him
a piece of broiled fish, and he took it and ate it in
their presence.*

"*He said to them, 'This is what I told you while I
was still with you: everything must be fulfilled
that is written about me in the Law of Moses, the
Prophets and the Psalms.'" (Luke 24 v 36-44)*

Jesus gave them, and he gives us, evidence—proof after
proof that it's really him, really risen. Just in that one
episode in that room, he appeared to them; he spoke
to them; he pointed to the nail-marks in his hands and
feet; he invited them to touch him to check; and then
he ate something. And he told them that what had
happened had been predicted hundreds of years before
by prophets like Isaiah—that he truly was, and is, the
one whom God had promised to send, the one who'd
been given to bring light to the darkness.

And that's just on this one occasion! Jesus was seen
and spoken to on numerous occasions, sometimes
by small groups and at least once by a gathering of
hundreds.

This is why the first followers of Jesus were willing to die for the claim that he was alive. They weren't just prepared to die for something they believed to be true, like martyrs of a religion or cause today; they were willing to die because of something they'd seen to be true. There's a big difference.

There's plenty more I could say about the evidence that Jesus really did rise from the dead: people have written whole books about it. But even after these few brief paragraphs, I hope you're beginning to see that it actually stacks up—that we're dealing with the realm of fact, not fairytale.

Here's another way to think about it. Ask yourself: is there a better historical explanation for the events of the first Easter Sunday that are uncontested?

First, there's the empty tomb. Not even Jesus' enemies denied at the time that the body was gone. So if Jesus did not rise again, where did his body go? If the authorities had taken it, surely they would have produced it when Jesus' friends started talking about a resurrection? If the disciples had taken it, surely at least one of them would have admitted it when they started being imprisoned, tortured and worse for their claims?

Second, there's the transformation in Jesus' followers and the explosive growth of Christianity in the 1st century. They went from a small crew of defeated, terrified men and women, cowering behind a locked door, to a rapidly growing network of groups confidently and joyfully talking about Jesus even when faced with death—so confidently and joyfully, in fact, that their teaching revolutionised first the eastern Mediterranean, then the Roman Empire, and, in time, the world, changing the way people thought about the value of life, the equality of all people, the nature of relationships, the way to use power... the list goes on.* What else could have caused that? What other explanation fits the facts so well?

My point is this: to believe in the resurrection is not to follow a preconception or prejudice—it is to follow the historical evidence. The Bible doesn't ask you to shut your eyes and make a leap of faith. Instead, it encourages you to open your eyes, look at the evidence, and make a step of faith. True faith is not believing something in spite of the evidence—it is believing something in spite of the consequences.

Because if this is true, then it's wonderful. It changes everything.

NEEDLE AND THREAD
If Jesus rose from the dead, then it is the ultimate proof that he really is the Mighty God and the Prince

---

* If you'd like to know more about how the values we all hold to today were prompted and shaped by the Christian message, a fascinating book to read is *The Air We Breathe* by Glen Scrivener (The Good Book Company, 2022).

of Peace whom Isaiah promised. And his resurrection is also significant because it hints at the third of the four titles Isaiah gave him. If Jesus came back from the dead, he's everlasting—and he offers to be our "Everlasting Father".

I don't know what kind of dad you have, or had. Maybe you had a great dad. Maybe yours just wasn't there, or if he was, you wished he hadn't been. But the image of the Everlasting Father—the image of any good father in the Bible—is of someone who sorts things out. They care for you and about you, they get things done, and they make sure their family's protected. That's what a dad should do, and so that's what the title "Everlasting Father" tells us about who Jesus is and what he does. He sorts out eternity, and he does so by sorting out the problem of death.

If Jesus got through death and into life beyond it, he can get me through it, too. In his resurrection, Jesus is like a needle that goes through a tapestry, and we're like the thread. He bursts through death and comes through the other side; and if we're attached to him, we follow through. Yes, we'll still die. But, like Jesus, we'll burst through into glorious new life on the other side.

Here, then, is the answer to death that we all need. With Jesus, death is not a dead end. It's a doorway, out into the paradise that Jesus promised that criminal as they hung on their crosses. Which means we don't have to downplay or deny or despair at death. Jesus has defeated death. His resurrection is a glimpse of the resurrection that each of us can experience, if we're attached to him. When, as a pastor, I lead a funeral, one of the most comforting, hope-filled moments is when I say at the start, "Jesus said, 'I am the resurrection and the life'"—because when Jesus said that, he was saying, *You can trust me with your death*.

REAL PURPOSE

But it's not just that. As our Everlasting Father, Jesus invites us to be part of the family business. He gives us work to do—work with an everlasting impact.

As I was catching up with that friend at our school reunion, it became clear that he'd been looking in all sorts of places for a sense of purpose, and that in the end it had all felt a bit pointless. Then it was time for me to share where life had taken me. It was at this point in the conversation that he shook his head and said, "I've spent my life just going from one thing to another. I've just lived." Then he added, "But you... you've had real purpose".

At the risk of sounding boastful, I can say that he's right. Not because I've done a better job than him of manufacturing a purpose for myself but because I'm a Christian—and Christians have been given the answer to that nagging question: "What is it all for?"

I remember the moment when I discovered it. Not long after I became a Christian, a friend showed me a verse from the Bible that totally changed my perspective. It's from part of the Bible where Paul, the writer, has just finished explaining about the evidence for the resurrection and how this guarantees that Christians will also live beyond death. Then he finishes by explaining how that hope for the future transforms what we do in the present:

> "Therefore, my dear brothers and sisters, stand firm. Let nothing move you. Always give yourselves fully to the work of the Lord, because you know that your labour in the Lord is not in vain."
>
> (1 Corinthians 15 v 58)

Reading that verse for the first time was a real light-bulb moment for me. Jesus' resurrection gave me hope in the face of death. And that meant that the idea of death no longer sapped life of all meaning. Nothing was in vain, and everything I did could be part of something that would last beyond my lifetime—the "work of the Lord". I had a purpose to live for because I had a person to live for: Jesus Christ—the Mighty God, Everlasting Father and Prince of Peace.

Jesus' resurrection means everything I do has meaning—not because of what I do but because of who I do it for. And Jesus extends that same invitation to you: to spend your life building something that lasts for ever. This sounds stark, but the truth is that if we find our significance in anything else, it will eventually let us down. But this won't. The resurrection is the great answer—the only answer—to John-Paul Sartre's claim that there is no reason for existing. The resurrection says that in fact there is a reason: it's to do things that matter for eternity—an eternity that anyone who trusts Jesus will themselves get to enjoy. Our lives can be more than a few short sentences in the great sweep of history; we won't be scrunched up and forgotten once we're gone, discarded as meaningless. Instead, our lives can have real meaning. When we live with Jesus as our Everlasting Father, all that we do with him and for him is woven into his bigger story—a story that does not end with death but only gets better beyond it.

5. CONFIDENCE

I love Christmas lights. The church I work for in the centre of London is yards from Oxford Street, one of the busiest shopping streets in the country—with a Christmas-lights budget to match. I love walking down it, looking up at the lights against the backdrop of the night sky while the shoppers and tourists and commuters bustle about below them.

The long-forgotten reason for the tradition of hanging lights in our streets, on our houses and on our trees each December is to remind us that Christmas is about a great light that came and shone against the backdrop of deep darkness. Every year at Christmas we hear those words from Isaiah in traditional carol services: "The people walking in darkness have seen a great light". Why? Because at the first Christmas, a child was born who was the Mighty God, the Prince of Peace and the Everlasting Father. Jesus gives hope, because he's the Mighty God, with the power to meet our deepest needs. Jesus offers peace, because he's the Prince of Peace, who tears down the barrier between us and God. And Jesus brings purpose, because he's the Everlasting Father, whose defeat of death gives life the meaning we long for.

So here's my question in this last chapter: will you ask Jesus to be for you the fourth description Isaiah gave him: your "Wonderful Counsellor"?

BETTER AND SAFER

Sometimes, life is confusing. We face decisions that we know will affect our lives in huge ways, and we don't know what route to take. We struggle with questions that we know matter greatly to ourselves and our loved ones, but our answers are only ever a best guess. We wrestle with a sense of regret at a path not taken. Life is often not a well-lit three-lane highway; it often feels like a dark country lane that we have to navigate without GPS.

In other words, we need what Isaiah would call a "counsellor": someone who directs you through life—the one you view as the authoritative expert, the person whose advice you always listen to. All of us treat someone as our counsellor: it may be a parent, a partner, a guru, a celebrity. Most often, it's simply ourselves—our own sense of what's right for us.

But there's no counsellor as wonderful as Jesus. After all, no one else understands this world better than the one who made it. No one else understands us as well as the one who formed us. No one else sees the future as clearly as the one who directs it. And no one else has proved themselves to be as trustworthy as the one who chose to be born into the mess of this world and to die on a cross simply because he loves us. Who else would be a better candidate to tell us how to walk through this life—in all its ups and downs, joys and sadnesses?

There's a great confidence to be enjoyed here. If Jesus is your counsellor, you no longer need to base your most important decisions on a best guess, whether yours or someone else's. You no longer need to lie awake worrying about taking a wrong turn. You no longer need to try to fake it till you make it, or hold the big questions at arm's length because you don't know how to answer them. You can simply let Jesus be God in your life. You can simply trust Jesus to be your Wonderful Counsellor. You can simply enjoy knowing that he knows what's best and can show you what's best as you seek to live life his way. And you can be sure that if you do mess things up, he'll be there, showing you how to pick up the pieces.

Living this way makes all the difference when things are dark. At the start of the Second World War, in 1939, as Britain faced Christmas with conflict raging and the future uncertain, King George VI, the father of Queen Elizabeth II, gave his traditional Christmas speech. He quoted from a poem by Minnie Louise Haskins:

> "And I said to the man who stood at the gate of the
> year:

> *'Give me a light that I may tread safely into the*
> *unknown.'*
> *And he replied:*
> *'Go out into the darkness and put your hand into*
> *the Hand of God.*
> *That shall be to you better than light and safer*
> *than a known way.'"*
>
> (God Knows, aka The Gate of the Year, 1912)

No one who puts their hand into Jesus' hand and asks him to lead them through the next year, through the whole of their life, and ultimately through their death, ever has reason to regret it.

THE GIFT YOU NEED

So here is the question to take away at the end of this book: what kind of gift do you think the baby born at the first Christmas really is?

Back in November 2010, one family received an early Christmas present when they sold a vase at auction that had been in the family for years and that they had recently inherited. It turned out it was a mid-18th-century Chinese Qianlong vase. When it came up for auction, it sold for £53 million. £53 million! One vase, worth millions.

When I heard about this, I became excited. My grandmother spent her childhood in Singapore, and she had left me a very old vase. Here was my ticket out of the rest of my working life! I started to look at the price of property in Bermuda. But then I actually asked someone who knows about these things how much my grandmother's vase was worth. They had a look—and told me its real value. Suffice to say, I still work six days a week, and we still haven't been to Bermuda.

Most people go through life thinking Jesus is like my vase. If he even existed at all, he's an irrelevance. His birth is an excuse to take a few days off and learn to pull fake smiles when we're given bubble bath we don't want or socks we don't need. And that's it.

But if Jesus is in fact the one whom Isaiah promised and who he himself claimed to be... if Jesus rose from the dead to prove it... then you are looking at a gift more like that Qianlong vase.

Perhaps you heard about him before, years ago, but never realised his worth. Perhaps he's been on the periphery of your thoughts for a long time, but you've never understood his value. But if Jesus is who he says he is, then he offers what no amount of money could ever buy. If he's the Mighty God, who can give us hope, the Prince of Peace, who can give us forgiveness, the Everlasting Father, who can give us purpose, and the Wonderful Counsellor, who can give us confidence in life... then he's the one that we've all, deep down, been searching for. He's the one we all truly need.

If you could have anything this Christmas, what would you ask for—what would be on your ultimate wishlist? My guess is that—more than any possession, more even than any change in circumstances—you'd love to enjoy a life of hope, peace, purpose, and confidence. You'll find all of these if you discover who the baby in the manger was, and is. And all you need to do with him is what you do with any present. Accept it, say thank you for it, and enjoy it.

> "To us a child is born,
> to us a son is given,
> and the government will be on his shoulders.
> And he will be called
> Wonderful Counsellor, Mighty God,
> Everlasting Father, Prince of Peace."

What do *you* want for Christmas?

WHAT NEXT?

Thanks for reading this far. As you finish, it's worth asking yourself: what next?

Maybe you would like to look at Jesus some more before you make your mind up about him. If that's you, I'd love you to do two things. First, read a Gospel, a historical account of Jesus' life—why not read the rest of Luke, the Gospel this book has focused on? Second, pray—speak to God and ask him, if he is there, to help you see the reality of who he is.

There are two other things you could do. Go to a website—christianityexplored.org allows you to keep thinking about Jesus in your own way, at your own pace. Or you could join an informal course based on the themes of this book, called Hope Explored, where you can hear more and ask questions, discuss or simply listen. You can find a course near you on that website.

Perhaps, though, you are at the point where you'd like to ask Jesus to be your Wonderful Counsellor—to help, forgive and lead you. Here are a few words that you could say to him now:

Jesus, I am accepting you, the Mighty God, as my Wonderful Counsellor. Thank you that you died to give me peace with you and rose again to give me an eternal life with you beyond death. I am sorry that I have not let you call the shots in my life. Thank you for forgiving me, and please help me live with you in charge of my decisions and my direction in life from now on. Amen.

Thanks again for reading. *Rico*

thegoodbook
COMPANY

Thanks for reading this book. We hope you enjoyed it, and found it helpful.

Most people want to find answers to the big questions of life: Who are we? Why are we here? How should we live? But for many valid reasons we are often unable to find the time or the right space to think positively and carefully about them.

Perhaps you have questions that you need an answer for. Perhaps you have met Christians who have seemed unsympathetic or incomprehensible. Or maybe you are someone who has grown up believing, but need help to make things a little clearer.

At The Good Book Company, we're passionate about producing materials that help people of all ages and stages understand the heart of the Christian message, which is found in the pages of the Bible.

Whoever you are, and wherever you are at when it comes to these big questions, we hope we can help. As a publisher we want to help you look at the good book that is the Bible because we're convinced that as we meet the person who stands at its heart—Jesus Christ—we find the clearest answers to our biggest questions.

Visit our website to discover the range of books, videos and other resources we produce, or visit our partner site www.christianityexplored.org for a clear explanation of who Jesus is and why he came.

Thanks again for reading,

Your friends at The Good Book Company

thegoodbook.com | thegoodbook.co.uk
thegoodbook.com.au | thegoodbook.co.nz | thegoodbook.co.in

WWW.CHRISTIANITYEXPLORED.ORG

Our partner site is a great place to explore the Christian faith, with powerful testimonies and answers to difficult questions.